W9-CBD-917

THE KENTUCKY BOURBON COCKTAIL BOOK

THE

KENTUCKY BOURBON

COCKTAIL BOOK

Joy Perrine and Susan Reigler

Photographs by Pam Spaulding

The University Press of Kentucky

Editorial and Sales Offices: The University Press of Kentucky
663 South Limestone Street, Lexington, Kentucky 40508–4008
www.kentuckypress.com

13 12 11 10 09 5 4 3 2

Library of Congress Cataloging-in-Publication Data

Perrine, Joy.
The Kentucky bourbon cocktail book / Joy Perrine and Susan Reigler ;
photographs by Pam Spaulding.
p. cm.
Includes index.
ISBN 978-0-8131-9246-8 (hardcover : alk. paper)
1. Cocktails.   2. Whiskey.   I. Reigler, Susan, 1955–   II. Title.
TX951.P474 2009
641.8'74—dc22   2009020115

This book is printed on acid-free paper meeting
the requirements of the American National Standard
for Permanence in Paper for Printed Library Materials.

Manufactured in Canada.

Member of the Association of
American University Presses

CONTENTS

PREFACE

by Susan Reigler

A few years ago, when asked to write an essay on bourbon for a Kentucky travel book, I expressed a strong opinion about how to drink Kentucky's amber elixir. While it is true that I enjoyed the occasional Manhattan or Old Fashioned, most of my bourbon drinking took the form of neat or with a splash of water. So I included the following sentences in my essay:

> *This author is occasionally asked by friends from other states about popular bourbon drinks. I tend to grow faint at the thought of "bourbon drinks" and must have a bracer in order to recover.*

It's never pleasant to have to eat one's words, but having to drink them is another, entirely enjoyable, matter altogether.

Not long after I so strongly expressed my bourbon sipping views, Jack's Lounge opened. Owned by award-winning chef Dean Corbett, whose restaurant, Equus, is just next door, its presiding mixologist was, and is, Joy Perrine, who was hired by Corbett in 1987. Joy, by her own admission, "loves to play with liquor" and loves using bourbon as a foundation to create new cocktails. She completely changed my mind about bourbon drinks.

I first visited Jack's as the restaurant critic and drinks writer for the Louisville *Courier-Journal.* Jack's is a bar for adults. It has upholstered armchairs and leather sofas. Conversation is the preferred form of entertainment. Every few weeks, Joy invents new drinks for the customers, many of whom are stalwart regulars. On an early visit, in the spirit of critiquing adventure, I sampled one of Joy's fruit-infused bourbon cocktails and recognized genius when I tasted it.

Happily, I have been able to sample many more over the years, including her many prize-winning drinks, such as the Spiceberry, included in this collection. Joy has been honored with *Louisville Magazine*'s "Best of" award as the city's best bartender.

This book came about because, as an admiring sipper, I asked Joy if she'd ever considered publishing a collection of her recipes. She responded with enthusiasm. Joy was annoyed that every bartending guide she'd every come across—and she has an extensive collection—folded bourbon into "whiskey drinks." She had long thought that bourbon deserved its own collection of drinks recipes. I volunteered to help her organize her recipes, and this is the result. It has been a true pleasure working with her to bring this collection to you.

If you are in Louisville and love a great cocktail, visit Jack's, 122 Sears Avenue, for one of her masterpieces. But if you can't make it to the Derby City, this book will be the next best thing. Happy shaking, stirring, and sipping!

CHAPTER ONE

Getting Started

Interest in bourbon, America's native spirit and a beverage almost exclusively distilled in Kentucky, has never been greater. Thanks in part to both the general popularity of cocktails and the marketing efforts of the bourbon distillers, there are now more brands of bourbons and more bourbon drinkers than ever. Even in New York, where the Manhattan is said to have been invented (using rye whiskey), when you order the hometown cocktail you'll be asked which *bourbon* you want in it.

Of course, the main reason bourbon is growing in popularity is that it tastes terrific. The dominant flavors in the whiskey, which must be distilled from a mixture of fermented grains containing at least 51 percent corn, are caramel and vanilla. Depending on other factors, such as yeast strains, proportions of barley and rye or wheat, and aging time, you may taste honey, toffee, citrus, and more—even chocolate. Not surprisingly, with the interest in bourbon, there's also an interest in how to drink it.

In addition to the snifter-worthy bourbons that are becoming popular as after-dinner libations in high-end restaurants, bartenders around the country are having fun finding new ways to mix the whiskey. It's obviously natural that a bartender who lives in Kentucky, where almost all bourbon is made, would be at the forefront of bourbon cocktail creativity.

Coincident with renewed interest in bourbon is a trend toward home entertaining, and that's why we've written this guide. It contains more than 100 of Joy's recipes, organized into chapters by drink genre. They range from her versions of the classic bourbon cocktails, such as the Old Fashioned and Mint Julep, to her trademark infusion drinks, many of which are among her award-winners.

If you're wondering about the concept of mixing bourbon with other ingredients, know that infusing bourbon with a variety of flavors has a long Kentucky history. Look at nineteenth- and early twentieth-century cookbooks and you'll find many recipes for punches and cordials using bourbon. Of all the bourbon served in Kentucky bars today, at least half is mixed with something. Coca-Cola, Diet Coke, ginger ale, 7UP, and club soda are the most popular mixers. I've just gone further and used all kinds of ingredients to mix with Kentucky bourbon.

Also included here are seasonal drinks, dessert drinks, and of course Derby cocktails. One chapter is devoted to "guest" drinks from my friends and colleagues. We have also provided suggestions for small bites to serve with your cocktails, as well as a glossary of bourbon terminology and a short list of suggested further reading about bourbon and bartending.

While many bartending guides include some bourbon cocktails, none has the range of drinks presented here. Joy has concocted simple-to-make recipes for the home bartender. Here's how to do it:

EQUIPMENT NEEDED

Shakers

Standard shaker made of stainless steel, *or*

Boston shaker, which has a stainless steel top half that fits over a glass
   bottom half or a drink glass. (Most home bartenders find the standard
   shaker easier to use.)

It is very important to have a large shaker with room for lots of ice; smaller ice cubes make a better drink and together should take up only about half of your shaker's volume. In the recipes that call for shaking, don't just tip the shaker back and forth. Shake vigorously. Be enthusiastic! The object is to chill the ingredients thoroughly, not to dilute them with melting ice. If your shaker frosts up, you are doing it right. Although professional bartenders may not use a towel, you'll be more comfortable holding the shaker with one during this process.

Measurers

4-ounce measured shot glass

8-ounce standard glass measuring cup

Strainer

Hawthorn bar strainer, flat, with
  a steel coil.

You can find these in any
kitchenware shop that carries
bar supplies. The strainer fits
over the rim of the glass. Pour
the chilled contents of the shaker
into the glass.

Muddler

A small wooden pestle used for
crushing fruits or herbs and
"muddling" them, as the name
suggests, with water and/or
sugar.

*Tools for the home bartender. Left to right: bottle
opener, strainer, muddler, metal bar spoon,
channel knife, zester, and wooden bar spoon,
arranged on a wooden cutting board.*

Long-handled Spoon

Great for stirring pitchers of drinks. Have both metal and wooden spoons on
hand.

Zester/Channel Knife

The gizmo you use to get twists of fruit peel, such as lemon or orange.

Glasses

Most of the recipes in this book call for either an Old Fashioned (also called rocks) glass or a Martini glass. A few need other types. The following icons indicate the glass required for each recipe:

Old Fashioned

Martini

Tall

Hurricane

Champagne flute

Wine glass

Shot glass

Stoneware mug

Pint beer glass

Punch cup

One other technique that you'll come across in some of my recipes is that of floating, or layering ingredients on top of one another. This requires no special equipment but takes a little more practice and a lot more finesse than shaking. The basic method is to hold a teaspoon, bowl side down, over the glass and slowly pour a thin stream of liquid over the back of the spoon so that it dribbles over the spoon edge and gently settles on top of the liquid already in the glass.

INGREDIENTS

Garnishes and Other Ingredients

You'll find a variety of these in this book's recipes. Always buy the best quality available. The basic ones are:

Red maraschino cherries
Oranges
Lemons
Angostura bitters

Bourbon

Feel free to use your favorite bourbon, but just so you know, my Bartender's Dozen bourbons, those I use most frequently in my cocktails, are:

Basil Hayden
Blanton
Buffalo Trace
Evan Williams Single Barrel
Four Roses Single Barrel
Jefferson Reserve
Jim Beam White Label
Maker's Mark
Old Fitzgerald Prime
Old Forester 86 proof
Pappy Van Winkle 15-year-old
Wild Turkey 80 proof
Woodford Reserve

I hope you'll enjoy using my recipes for Kentucky bourbon cocktails at home. I created these drinks to be fun and easy to make and to taste good. I have specified certain brands in my recipes because they make the drinks taste the way I want. If you use those specific labels, your cocktails will taste most like the ones served at Jack's. In recipes I entered in contests sponsored by particular distilleries, I obviously used their brands of liquor. But don't let that inhibit your creativity. Just as you should feel free to use your favorite bourbon, feel free also to use your favorite brands of mixers and other ingredients and to play with a recipe and make it your own. If it's too sweet, use less sugar. Too sour, add a little more sugar. Too strong, add a little water. And certainly, if you don't like it straight up, drink it on the rocks. There should be a little magic in every drink you pour, too. That will be your pleasure in mixing and serving good drinks to good friends.

Finally, I have a request based on many, many years of bartending. Please enjoy my creations responsibly. Drink in moderation and please, please, do not drink and drive.

CHAPTER TWO

Infusions

In this chapter, you'll be introduced to infusions, since the recipes here and several in later chapters (but certainly not all) call for infused bourbon. You might want to browse through the recipes, find which ones appeal to your taste, and start with one or two infusions. You'll also find here lists of garnishes and other ingredients for most of the drinks in this book.

Infusions are really quite easy to make. You are simply introducing a new flavor or bringing out a flavor already present and making those tastes *pop*. Kentucky bourbon is ideal for infusions because so many complex flavors are already in the whiskey. Sometimes these flavors just need some help to stand out and shout. As fascinating as the flavor changes brought about by infusions are, the color taken on by the liquor may be even more interesting. Depending on what you use to infuse it, the brown liquor can achieve a rainbow of colors as well as flavors.

Most infusions take about three days of steeping to develop their full flavor. At the end of that time, the bourbon is strained off, bottled, labeled, dated, and put in the refrigerator. Some infusions will keep for years. My infusions are made to sell at Jack's—and they go quickly—so I'm always both infusing tested recipes and trying new ones.

I use fresh, ripe fruit and clear glass jars so I can see what's happening during the process. I love to use fruits in season and tie in holiday flavors when possible. The difficult part comes when I'm satisfied with the infusion. It's now time to invent the cocktail using the infusion as the base. But this is also a lot of fun.

Many factors go into creating a cocktail, including flavor (sweet, savory, or spicy), the season or special event (such as Christmas or Derby), and the overall character of the drink (refreshing, light, warm, comforting, exotic). Try to think outside the bottle and inside the glass.

Next comes the garnish—simple or over the top—and then, finally, the name. Your cocktail creations are a little like your children, and they need to be named.

EQUIPMENT NEEDED

1-liter bottle of Kentucky bourbon (of your choice)
Clean, clear 2-gallon or 1-gallon glass jar with a plastic lid
Pitcher (glass, half-gallon)

Mesh strainer that will fit over the top
of the pitcher
Coffee filters (Mr. Coffee or Melitta
No. 4)
Long-handled wooden spoon
Funnel
Bottle and cap for the finished product
(may be the empty bottle from the
bourbon used in the recipe)
Stick-on labels for the name of the
infusion ingredients and the date
made

*Vessels. Left to right: large standard
shaker, mesh strainer with coffee filters,
lidded jar for infusions, Boston shaker,
small standard shaker, and glass pitcher
for punches.*

SUGGESTED INFUSION
INGREDIENTS

Fruits

Berries: strawberries, blackberries, blueberries, or raspberries

Cherries (sweet pitted)

Pineapple (peeled and cored)

Citrus fruits: lemons, blood oranges, Cara Cara oranges, ruby red grapefruit
(peel and fruit only; the white pith would make the infusion too bitter),
limes (again, peel and fruit only), key limes

Cranberries
Red or green apples (seeded and cored)
Plums (stones removed)
Peaches (peeled and stones removed)
Red or green pears (seeded and cored)
Star fruit (sliced)

Herbs and Spices
Ginger root (peeled)
Vanilla beans (seeds only, not pod)
Fresh mint (Kentucky Colonel, spearmint, peppermint, chocolate mint, or lemon mint)
Star anise—whole
Ground cinnamon, allspice, mace, ginger, nutmeg, and clove
Hot peppers (jalapeño, serrano, habanero), seeded and sliced

Sweets
Candy canes (red and white only; green will color the mixture)
Rock candy

This is just a basic list. As you experiment with your own creations, you'll no doubt discover more intriguing ingredients to add to your infusion jars.

INFUSION RECIPES

For all infusions, you'll need the equipment listed above (pages 10–11). Each recipe calls for a 1-liter bottle of the Kentucky bourbon of your choice.

When using fruit, always wash it before using it. Most of the fruits left over after making the infusion can be used in making sorbet. But *do not* heat them on the stovetop, since the bourbon-soaked pulp will be highly flammable! You could add sugar to the leftover fruit and pour it over vanilla ice cream for a very grown-up sundae.

SPICE (Six-Spice Mix)

Combine equal parts of the following in covered container and mix well.

Ground allspice
Ground cloves
Ground mace
Ground nutmeg
Ground ginger
Ground cinnamon

Pour the bourbon into the glass jar and add 2 tablespoons of the spice mix. Shake and let steep for 3 days. Strain into the empty bourbon bottle. Label, date, and refrigerate.

APPLE PEAR SPICE

1 teaspoon six-spice mix (above)
1 red apple
1 green apple
1 pear

Core and slice the fruit. Combine with bourbon and let steep for 5 days. Strain into the empty bourbon bottle. Label, date, and refrigerate.

BLACKBERRY

1 pint ripe blackberries

Lightly crush about a third of the berries and combine all fruit with the bourbon. Shake and let steep 3 days. Strain, label, date, and refrigerate.

BLOOD ORANGE
(usually available around Christmas)

4 ripe blood oranges, cut in half, then sliced

Combine fruit with bourbon. Shake and let steep 3 days. Strain, label, date, and refrigerate.

BLUEBERRY

1 pint ripe blueberries

Lightly crush a third of the berries and combine all fruit with bourbon. Shake and let steep 3 days. Strain, label, date, and refrigerate.

CANDY CANE

12 red and white 5-inch peppermint candy canes broken into small pieces

Don't use candy canes with green in them because they give the bourbon an unattractive murky green color. Add the candy pieces to the bourbon and let steep 1 day. Pour into the bourbon bottle (no need to strain). Label, date, and refrigerate.

CARA CARA ORANGE

3 medium Cara Cara oranges, sliced

This is a very sweet orange variety with pinkish flesh and a honey flavor. Add the fruit to the bourbon and let steep for 3 days. Strain, label, date, and refrigerate.

CINNAMON

2 tablespoons ground cinnamon

Combine cinnamon and bourbon. Shake and let steep 3 days. Strain, label, date, and refrigerate.

CRANBERRY ORANGE

1 bag (about 1 pound) fresh cranberries, washed and picked through
thinly sliced zest from 1 orange

Crush about a third of the berries and add all ingredients to the glass jar. Let steep 5 days. Strain, label, date, and refrigerate.

KEY LIME

10 small key limes, cut into wedges

Add fruit to bourbon and steep 3 days. Strain, label, date, and refrigerate.

LEMON

6 lemons, each cut into 6 wedges

Squeeze and drop 12 of the wedges into the glass jar. Add other wedges without squeezing. Shake and steep 3 days. Strain, label, date, and refrigerate. Discard the used lemons.

PEACH

6 medium-size ripe summer
    peaches, peeled, pitted, and sliced

This is a very seasonal preparation, a true taste of summer. Combine with bourbon and steep 3 days. Strain, label, date, and refrigerate.

PINEAPPLE

1 ripe pineapple, peeled, cored, and diced
1 teaspoon six-spice mix (above)

Do not use canned pineapple. Add the fruit to the bourbon and steep 3 days. Strain, label, date, and refrigerate.

Infusions in champagne flutes. Left to right: Spice, Pineapple, Blueberry, Blackberry, and Strawberry.

RUBY RED GRAPEFRUIT

2 ruby red grapefruit

Peel the skin, leaving the white pith on the fruit, and cut the peel into thin slices. Remove the pith from the fruit, discard it (the pith would make the infusion bitter), and cut the fruit into segments. Combine peel, fruit, and bourbon. Shake and steep 3 days. Strain, label, date, and refrigerate.

STRAWBERRY

1 pint fresh ripe strawberries, cleaned, stemmed, and sliced

Combine fruit and bourbon. Shake and steep 3 days. Strain, label, date, and refrigerate.

SWEET SYRUPS

SIMPLE SYRUP (and Sweet and Sour Mix)

This is the basic syrup for classics such as the Old Fashioned and the Mint Julep, as well as for many of my original bourbon cocktails.

2 cups white sugar
1 cup boiling water

Add sugar to water and stir
until completely dissolved.
Let cool. Bottle, label, and
refrigerate.
   To make fresh sweet and
sour mix, add 2 parts fresh-
squeezed lemon juice to 1
part simple syrup.

Assorted syrups.

BROWN SUGAR SYRUP

2 cups light brown sugar (Do not use dark brown; the flavor overwhelms
   drinks.)
1 cup boiling water

Add sugar to water and stir until completely dissolved. Let cool. Bottle, label,
and refrigerate.

HONEY OR SORGHUM

Combine equal parts honey or sorghum and hot water; stir to dissolve, and cool. Make as needed. The flavor goes off in stored syrup.

MAPLE

The easiest "recipe" in this book. Just use pure maple syrup straight from the bottle.

GARNISHES

Garnishes add an extra dimension of visual fun to your drinks. Whether simply pretty or outright eye-catching, they usually reflect an ingredient already in the cocktail. If added for purely visual effect, a garnish should not affect the taste of the drink.

Fruits and Spices
Lime, lemon, orange, or grapefruit in wedges, wheels, or twists
Pineapple
Apple, pear, peach, or star fruit in slices
Blackberries, blueberries, raspberries, strawberries

Sugarcane sticks, cinnamon sticks
Grapes; canned sweet pitted
    cherries, drained and rinsed;
    green cherries (not flavored)

Savory
Black olives (canned)
Asparagus
Carrot curls
Cherry peppers
Baby corn
Celery sticks

Mint
There are many mint cultivars.
The variety of spearmint known
as Kentucky Colonel is my
favorite for Mint Juleps. Other
mints that add interesting flavor
accents to my drinks are apple
mint, chocolate mint, cinnamon
mint, orange mint, peppermint,
pineapple mint, spearmint, and
Sweet Melissa/lemon mint.

Fruit and vegetables suitable for garnish.

INFUSION DRINKS

BLUE MOON OVER KENTUCKY

2 ounces blueberry-infused bourbon
1 ounce limoncello
1 teaspoon simple syrup
1 large lemon wedge

Combine over ice; squeeze and drop the lemon wedge into the ingredients. Strain into a chilled glass and garnish with a thin slice of lemon floated on top of the drink.

CARA CARA ORANGE SOUR

2 ounces Cara Cara orange–infused bourbon
1 tablespoon brown sugar syrup
1 ounce orangecello

Shake over ice and strain into a chilled glass. Garnish with a large Cara Cara orange wedge on the rim.

HARVEST MOON

1½ ounces spice-infused bourbon
¾ ounce DeKuyper ButterShots (butterscotch schnapps)
¾ ounce praline liqueur
1 ounce Baileys Irish Cream

Combine over ice and strain into a chilled glass. Sprinkle with ground nutmeg.

KENTUCKY BOURBON KEY LIME SOUR

2 ounces key lime–infused bourbon
1 tablespoon simple syrup
1 teaspoon Stirrings Clarified Key Lime
1 tablespoon fresh key lime juice

Shake over ice and strain into a glass. Garnish with a thin wheel of key lime on the rim or floating on top of the drink.

PEACH MANHATTAN

2 ounces peach-infused bourbon
2 ounces Noilly Prat dry vermouth
4–5 dashes Fee Brothers peach bitters

Shake over ice and strain into the chilled glass. Garnish with a large peach wedge on the rim of the glass.

SOUTHERN PEACH SOUR

2 ounces peach-infused bourbon
1 tablespoon brown sugar syrup
1 ounce fresh lemon juice

Shake over ice and strain into the glass. Garnish with a large wedge of fresh peach.

Summer Manhattans. Strawberry (left),
Blueberry (foreground), and Blackberry (rear).

SUMMER FRUIT MANHATTANS

2 ounces blackberry- ,
    blueberry- , or strawberry-
    infused bourbon
½ ounce Noilly Prat sweet
    vermouth
4–5 dashes Angostura bitters

Shake over ice and strain into
a chilled glass. Garnish with
3 blackberries on a pick, 5
blueberries on a pick, or a large
strawberry on the rim of the glass.

2 ounces of blackberry- , blueberry- , or strawberry-infused bourbon
1 tablespoon brown sugar syrup
1 tablespoon blackberry, blueberry, or strawberry syrup (I prefer Smucker's)
1 ounce fresh lemon juice

Combine and shake over ice. Strain and pour into a large Old Fashioned glass. Drop in 3 blackberries or 5 blueberries, or garnish with a large strawberry on the rim of the glass.

CHAPTER THREE

The Classics

The most famous bourbon cocktails are certainly the Old Fashioned and the Manhattan. The Old Fashioned was first mixed at Louisville's Pendennis Club in the 1880s for a member, a retired Civil War officer, who didn't like the taste of bourbon. He did, however, want to stay on the good side of the distillery owners who were his fellow members. So the bartender came up with the eminently palatable Old Fashioned. (This has also been my philosophy in concocting bourbon cocktails—to allow people to enjoy bourbon who thought they didn't like it!) Eventually, like the Martini, the Old Fashioned even spawned its own eponymous glass. The squat bar glass came to be called an Old Fashioned glass.

The Manhattan also has a colorful tale attached to it. The popular version is that it was created in 1874 at New York City's Manhattan Club at an event hosted by Lady Jennie Churchill, American wife of British parliamentarian Lord Randolph Churchill, the parents of future Prime Minister Winston Churchill. The soiree was held in honor of New York's newly elected governor, Samuel J. Tilden. Or not. There are also some indications that a Manhattan-like cocktail was being served several years before this.

In addition to the Old Fashioned and the Manhattan, we've included my takes on other bourbon drinks that have attained the status of classics—the Hot Toddy, John Collins, Mint Julep, Sazerac, and Whiskey Sour.

OLD FASHIONED

1 tablespoon simple syrup
6 dashes Angostura bitters
1 orange wedge
1 red cherry
2 ounces water
2 ounces Kentucky bourbon

Put the simple syrup and bitters in the glass. Add orange wedge and cherry; muddle. Add ice, water, and bourbon, and stir. Garnish with a long-stem cherry.

ORIGINAL MANHATTAN

For each version of the Manhattan, combine bourbon, vermouth, and bitters over ice and shake. Strain into a chilled glass. Nothing ruins a Manhattan faster than old or cheap vermouth. Use Noilly Prat vermouths from France and buy the small bottles. Yes, the traditional Manhattan has bitters in it.

2 ounces Kentucky bourbon
¼ ounce Noilly Prat sweet
   vermouth
4 dashes Angostura bitters

Garnish with a red cherry.

The Classics. Whiskey Sour (left), John Collins (right), Old Fashioned (foreground), and Manhattan (background).

DRY MANHATTAN

2 ounces Kentucky bourbon
¼ ounce Noilly Prat dry vermouth

See note under Original Manhattan, previous page. Garnish with a large green pitted olive.

PERFECT MANHATTAN

2 ounces Kentucky bourbon
¼ ounce Noilly Prat dry vermouth
¼ ounce Noilly Prat sweet vermouth
3–4 dashes Angostura bitters

See note under Original Manhattan, previous page. Garnish with a large lemon twist.

HOT TODDY MUG

This is the favorite way to take the chill off during a damp, chilly Kentucky winter. An armchair beside a blazing fireplace is a pleasant optional ingredient.

5 ounces hot water just off the boil
2 ounces Kentucky bourbon
1 tablespoon simple syrup
lemon twist

Pour hot water into an 8–9 ounce stoneware mug. Add bourbon, syrup, and a lemon twist.

JOHN COLLINS

This variation on the gin-based Tom Collins takes its name from "John Barleycorn," a traditional nickname for bourbon.

2 ounces Kentucky bourbon
$\frac{1}{2}$ ounce simple syrup
1 ounce sweet and sour mix
2 ounces club soda

To a glass filled with ice, add bourbon, syrup, and sweet and sour mix; shake. Add club soda. Squeeze and drop a large lemon wedge into the glass. Add a long straw and a cherry.

MINT JULEP

A sterling silver julep cup is the ultimate vessel in which to serve this classic. The next best is one of the official souvenir glasses made each year for the Kentucky Derby. These glasses are readily available in liquor stores in the Louisville area starting in March and are sold until the year's supply runs out. My collection of Derby glasses dates back to 1969, the year my daughter was born.

1 ounce simple syrup
5–7 mint leaves (Kentucky Colonel variety if available)
3 ounces Kentucky bourbon
3 ounces water

Into a large mixing glass pour simple syrup, add mint, and muddle well. Add bourbon and water. Fill with crushed ice or small ice cubes, and shake. Garnish with a large sprig of fresh mint and add a long straw.

SAZERAC

This potent classic takes its name from the Sazerac Coffee House in New Orleans, where it was first served.

1 teaspoon Pernod
2 ounces Kentucky bourbon
1 tablespoon simple syrup
6 dashes Peychaud's bitters

Pour Pernod into the glass and swirl to coat. Pour out the excess. Add ice, bourbon, syrup, and bitters; shake. Garnish with a large lemon twist.

WHISKEY SOUR

Sometime in the mid-nineteenth century, bartenders started doctoring bourbon and rye with lemon juice, and "sour" drinks were born. The citrus employed here is orange.

2 ounces Kentucky bourbon
1 tablespoon simple syrup
1 ounce sweet and sour mix
½ ounce fresh orange juice

In a glass filled with ice, combine all ingredients; shake. Garnish with an orange wheel and a cherry.

CHAPTER FOUR

Joy's Award-Winning Bourbon Cocktails

BOURBONBALL
(Tuaca Cocktail Contest, 2001. First Place)

When Jack's Lounge opened in 2000, I wanted a signature drink. I thought it should use bourbon as a base and be a little different. I love bourbon ball candy and didn't think anyone else was doing this kind of drink. The result was the first drink creation of mine to win national attention. There are people who come to Jack's specifically to have a Bourbonball.

1 part Woodford Reserve
1 part Tuaca
1 part dark crème de cacao

Combine, shake over ice, and
strain into a chilled glass.
Garnish with a strawberry on
the rim.

The Bourbonball in a Martini glass.

The Manhattan Italiano in a champagne flute.

MANHATTAN ITALIANO
(Woodford Reserve Manhattan
Contest, 2008. Second Place)

I wanted to do something different using bourbon, bitters, and wine to make a summer drink. Originally I used Stirrings' Blood Orange Bitters, but that product has become hard to find, so I switched to Fee Brothers or Regan's.

2 ounces Woodford Reserve
1/2 ounce Tuaca
1/2 ounce triple sec
6 dashes Fee Brothers West Indian
    orange bitters or Regan's No. 6
    orange bitters
1/2 ounce Cinzano Bianco (white sweet
    vermouth)

Combine, shake over ice, and strain into a chilled glass. Garnish with an orange slice and a large black pitted olive on a pick.

THE KENTUCKY BOURBON COCKTAIL BOOK

The Spiceberry with starfruit garnish in a tall glass.

SPICEBERRY
(Woodford Reserve Infusion
Contest, 2006. First Place)

*This is my drink for the holidays,
Thanksgiving through Christmas, using the
holiday flavors of spices and cranberries.
The resulting color reminds me of the
berries of the spiceberry tree, which are
used throughout Kentucky in seasonal
decorations.*

1 part spice-infused Woodford
   Reserve
1 part Tuaca
1 part cranberry juice

Combine, shake over ice, and strain into
a chilled glass. Garnish with half an
orange slice and three fresh cranberries
on a pick.

TROPICALE

(Woodford Reserve Infusion Contest, 2007.
Third Place)

When I taste Woodford Reserve, I get hints of pineapple, coconut, brown sugar, and spice, so I thought I could make a tropical cocktail with the bourbon. It works chilled (without ice), over ice, by the pitcher, or even as a hot drink. (Heat only the pineapple juice, not the liquors.) We sell a huge amount of the chilled version at Jack's during the summer, and we do the hot version in winter.

1½ ounces pineapple- and spice-infused Woodford Reserve
¾ ounce Cruzan coconut rum
¾ ounce Tuaca
1 tablespoon brown sugar syrup
2 ounces pineapple juice

Combine, shake over ice, and strain into a chilled glass. Garnish with a red cherry (no stem) dropped in the drink, and a pineapple wedge on the rim. Or you can serve over ice in a tall glass with the same garnish.

For the hot version, shake other ingredients (without ice) and add to pineapple juice warmed in a heat-proof glass mug. Sprinkle with ground nutmeg.

The Tropicale with pineapple, orange, starfruit, and green cherry garnish.

CHAPTER FIVE

Bourbon Cocktails by the Calendar

COCKTAILS FOR ALL SEASONS (Sip any time!)

AMERICAN COCKTAIL

2 ounces Kentucky bourbon (80–90 proof)
¾ ounce pure maple syrup
1 ounce fresh orange juice
1 ounce cranberry juice
1 tablespoon fresh lemon juice

Combine and shake over ice. Strain into a chilled glass and garnish with a large orange twist.

BEE STING

2 ounces Wild Turkey 101
1 ounce Wild Turkey American Honey Liqueur
1 ounce sweet and sour mix

Combine and shake over ice. Strain into a chilled glass. Squeeze a lemon wedge into the glass and drop it in to garnish.

FRENCH MANHATTAN

2 ounces Kentucky bourbon
¾ ounce Chambord
½ ounce Noilly Prat sweet vermouth
3–4 dashes Angostura bitters

Combine and shake over ice. Strain into a chilled glass and garnish with 3 fresh raspberries on a pick.

ITALIAN MANHATTAN

2 ounces Kentucky bourbon
¾ ounce Tuaca
½ ounce Noilly Prat dry vermouth
3–4 dashes Peychaud's bitters

Combine and shake over ice. Strain into a chilled glass and garnish with a large orange twist or orange slice on the rim.

KENTUCKY JELLYBEAN 101

When I first moved to Louisville in 1978, almost every bar in town did a Jellybean with various recipes topped with rum and then set on fire. This is my version, but no flames, please. I saw too many people accidentally set themselves on fire!

⅓ ounce grenadine
⅓ ounce green crème de menthe
⅓ ounce anisette
⅓ ounce blackberry brandy
⅓ ounce Wild Turkey 101

Into a 2-ounce fluted shot glass, starting with the grenadine, pour each of the ingredients, in the order listed, over the back of a spoon, making a layer with each.

KENTUCKY PEACH MELBA

1½ ounces Kentucky bourbon (80–90 proof)
1 ounce DeKuyper Peachtree schnapps
1 ounce Chambord
1 ounce Baileys Irish Cream

Combine, shake over ice, and strain into a chilled glass. Garnish with a fresh peach slice on the rim and 3 raspberries on a pick.

LOUISVILLE COCKTAIL

2 ounces Kentucky bourbon of your choice
½ ounce Lillet rouge
½ ounce Lillet blanc

Combine and shake over ice; strain into a chilled glass. Garnish with a large orange twist.

2 ounces Wild Turkey 101
1 ounce Rumple Minze peppermint schnapps

Combine and shake over ice. Strain into a glass filled with ice.

NEW WAVE COCKTAILS

These next two drinks provide a way to get your daily veggies. The preparation is a little more time-consuming, but you'll certainly impress the guests to whom you serve them.

SWEET POTATO PIE

The sweet potato pieces cup the drink. Eating them after you sip the liquid means that this is drink and dessert in one!

1 small sweet potato
sorghum syrup
chopped, toasted pecans
1 ounce spice-infused Kentucky bourbon
½ ounce brown sugar syrup
½ ounce pecan liqueur

Prepare the sweet potato as follows: Boil the potato until cooked but still firm. Cool and peel it and cut crosswise into three chunks. Scoop out the center of each piece, being careful not to scoop all the way through, making a "well" to hold the drink. Dip the potato rim in sorghum syrup and then in chopped, toasted pecans. Put ½ ounce sorghum in the bottom of a Martini glass and sprinkle with pecans. Place the three pieces of sweet potato into the Martini glass, hollowed-out centers facing up.

Shake the bourbon, brown sugar syrup, and pecan liqueur over ice and carefully pour into the sweet potato cups. Garnish with a dollop of whipped cream. Serve with two small sip straws and a small spoon. Sip the cocktail and eat the sweet potato pieces.

VEGGIE IMPLOSIONS

1 recipe Dark & Bloody Bourbon Mary (see p. 48)
assortment of vegetables, including
  cherry tomatoes
  cucumber pieces
  zucchini, uncooked
  summer squash, uncooked
  new potatoes, cooked

Carefully shave flesh from the base of the vegetable pieces so that they rest level on a tray or plate. Hollow out the inside of the vegetable pieces to make veggie "shot glasses." Place small bowls of condiments such as those produced by Bourbon Barrel Foods (BBF)—Bourbon Barrel Aged Soy Sauce, Bourbon Barrel Smoked Sea Salt, and Bourbon Barrel Smoked Peppercorns—around the veggies. Dip the rim of the veggie shots into the soy sauce, salt, and peppercorns.

Shake the Bloody Bourbon Mary mix over ice, strain into a small plastic squirt bottle, and squirt the Bloody Bourbon Mary mix into the shots. To enjoy, sip the drink and munch on the "shot glasses."

(For more information about BBF, go to www.bourbonbarrelfoods.com. You can order these ingredients online or by phone.)

DERBY DRINKS

Many places have four seasons—spring, summer, fall, winter. Louisville has a fifth. It's called Derby. Not surprisingly, the week before the Kentucky Derby (held the first Saturday in May), as well as Derby weekend itself, is a very busy time at Jack's Lounge. I have created several specialty drinks for horse racing fans and other people who simply love this great excuse for a party.

CHOCOLATE JULEP

I love this drink—Kentucky bourbon, mint, chocolate. A simple drink that says so much.

1 part Kentucky bourbon (80–90 proof)
1 part white crème de menthe
1 part Godiva chocolate liqueur

Combine and shake over ice; strain into a chilled glass. Garnish with a sprig of fresh chocolate mint.

This is the perfect drink for a Derby brunch. I relished rising to the challenge from those who said a Bloody Mary couldn't be made with bourbon. Ha!

1 teaspoon salt/pepper/paprika mix
2 ounces Kentucky bourbon
2 large lemon wedges
1 tablespoon Bourbon Barrel Aged Worcestershire Sauce
1 can (6 ounces) Campbell's tomato juice

To prepare the seasoning mix, combine in a mortar one part each smoked sea salt and smoked pepper and two parts smoked paprika, all from Bourbon Barrel Foods (www.bourbonbarrelfoods.com). Finely crush with a pestle and shake together in a jar.

To a pint glass or large mason jar filled with ice, add the bourbon, squeeze and drop in the lemon wedges, and add the teaspoon of seasoning mix and the Worcestershire sauce. Shake. Add more ice and the can of tomato juice. Shake again. Garnish with a long straw, baby corn, a large pitted black olive, and a cherry pepper, all on a stick.

The Dark & Bloody Bourbon Mary in a pint glass with vegetable garnish.

This is my version of that beloved southern beverage, sweet tea, so I suggest serving it in small Mason jars.

1 cup Kentucky bourbon
   (80–90 proof)
½ cup brown sugar syrup
½ cup DeKuyper Wild Strawberry
   liqueur
1 cup cooled tea
12 large lemon wedges
12 fresh strawberries, stemmed
   and sliced
½ cup sparkling wine

In a 1½ quart glass pitcher, combine the bourbon, brown sugar syrup, Wild Strawberry liqueur, and tea. Squeeze and drop in the lemon wedges, and stir well. Add ice cubes and strawberry slices. Top with sparkling wine, stir again, and serve.

Derby punch in a glass pitcher.

JULEP MANHATTAN

2 ounces Kentucky bourbon (80–90 proof)
¼ ounce white crème de menthe
¼ ounce Noilly Prat dry vermouth
3–4 drops Angostura bitters

Combine, shake over ice, and strain into a chilled Martini glass. Garnish with a sprig of fresh mint.

KENTUCKY COLONEL

1½ ounces Kentucky bourbon
½ ounce praline liqueur
½ ounce green crème de menthe
½ ounce white crème de cacao
¾ ounce Baileys Irish Cream

Combine, shake over ice, and strain into a chilled glass. Garnish with 3–4 leaves of fresh mint floating on the top of the drink.

KENTUCKY DERBY PIE

1½ ounces Kentucky bourbon (80–90 proof)
¾ ounce Nocello (walnut liqueur)
½ ounce Tuaca
¾ ounce Godiva chocolate liqueur
¾ ounce Baileys Irish Cream

Combine ingredients, shake over ice, and strain into a chilled glass. Sprinkle cocoa powder on top.

NEW FASHIONED

¾ ounce limoncello
6 dashes Angostura bitters
3 lemon wedges
2 cherries
2 ounces Kentucky bourbon
1 ounce Korbel Natural sparkling wine

In the bottom of the glass, put the limoncello and bitters. Squeeze and drop in the lemon wedges and add the cherries. Muddle. Add ice and bourbon, and shake. Add the Korbel. Serve with a short straw and garnish with a large lemon twist.

2 cups Kentucky bourbon (80–90 proof)
½ cup simple syrup
3 tablespoons Angostura bitters
1 cup fresh orange juice
½ cup fresh lemon juice
1 cup water

In a 1½–2 quart glass pitcher, combine all ingredients and stir well. Add ice and 20 stemmed red cherries, 12 orange half wheels, and small slices of star fruit.

PEACH JULEP

½ ounce brown sugar syrup
1½ ounces Monin peach syrup
5 mint leaves
3 slices fresh ripe, peeled peach
2 ounces Kentucky bourbon (80–90 proof)
2 ounces water

In a pint glass, gently muddle syrups, mint leaves, and peach slices. Add bourbon, water, and ice. Shake. Garnish with a large peach slice and a mint sprig. Serve with a long straw.

This is a cocktail buffet where everyone mixes his or her own drink. My inspiration for this setup came from time spent in the West Indies, where similar buffets are served using rum.

1 cup Kentucky bourbon (80–90 proof)
1 cup simple syrup
1 cup brown sugar syrup
1 cup water
1 small bottle Angostura bitters
cherries and wedges of lemon, lime, and orange

Put each of the liquid ingredients in its own pint glass carafe or pitcher, and each of the fruits in its own small glass bowl. Provide glasses, ice, and stir sticks. Sugar cane sticks add a festive touch used in place of the stir sticks.

SAUCY KENTUCKY BOURBON PUNCH

This punch is based on a recipe in the Courier-Journal Cookbook *(1971) for a sauce to serve over ice cream or cake. I loved the ingredients and thought they'd make a great drink. And they do!*

2 ounces Kentucky bourbon (80–90 proof)
1 ounce brown sugar syrup
1 ounce Smucker's strawberry syrup
1 ounce fresh orange juice
1 ounce fresh lemon juice
1 ounce praline liqueur

To a pint glass filled with ice, add all ingredients and shake. Garnish with a fresh strawberry and a lemon wheel on the rim. Serve with a long straw.

SPRING COCKTAILS

CHOCOLATE DROP

This is a perfect sip to take the spring chill off and toast the snowdrops popping up out of the ground.

1½ ounces Kentucky bourbon (80–90 proof)
¾ ounce Tuaca
1 teaspoon brown sugar syrup
¾ ounce Godiva chocolate liqueur
2 ounces half & half
1–2 ounces club soda

Shake all ingredients except the club soda over ice. Add more ice if needed and the soda. Stir. Sprinkle cocoa on top. Serve with a long straw.

EGG CREAM

1½ ounces Kentucky bourbon of your choice
¾ ounce Tuaca
1 teaspoon brown sugar syrup
2 ounces half & half
1–2 ounces club soda

Shake all ingredients except the club soda over ice and strain into a glass. Add more ice if needed and the soda. Stir and serve with a long straw. For a festive touch, add a few drops of red, blue, green, or yellow food coloring to the drink. Voila! Easter Egg Cream. Consider serving at an Easter brunch.

KENTUCKY SUNSHINE

2 ounces Kentucky sourwood honey dissolved in 2 ounces hot water
2 ounces Kentucky bourbon (80–90 proof)
2 ounces fresh lemon juice
2 ounces fresh orange juice
1 ounce medium dry sherry
1 ounce sparkling wine

Dissolve the honey in the hot water; otherwise it will not dissolve in the liquor. To an ice-filled glass, add all ingredients except the sparkling wine; shake. Add more ice if needed and the sparkling wine. Garnish with a drizzle of undiluted sourwood honey, a sprinkle of nutmeg, and a lemon wheel on the rim. Serve with a long straw.

SWEET MELISSA

This drink in named in honor of my daughter, Melissa, and the lemon honey candy we always buy when we visit the bee exhibit at the Kentucky State Fair.

2 ounces Kentucky bourbon (80–90 proof)
2 ounces sourwood honey dissolved in 2 ounces hot water and cooled
juice of half a lemon

Combine, shake over ice, and strain into a chilled glass. Garnish with a lemon wheel and a spring of lemon mint (also known as Sweet Melissa).

TORNADO

or

This is my Bluegrass version of the Hurricane, since Kentucky's strong wind storms are tornadoes.

2 ounces Kentucky bourbon (100 proof)
½ ounce simple syrup

1 ounce grenadine

1 ounce Rose's lime juice

1 ounce fresh orange juice

1 ounce passion fruit rum

Combine, shake over ice, and pour into a glass. Garnish with an orange wheel and a cherry. Serve with a long straw.

SUMMER COCKTAILS

BEE STINGER

1½ ounces Wild Turkey 101

¾ ounce Wild Turkey American Honey Liqueur

¾ ounce limoncello

Combine all ingredients over ice in the glass, and shake. Garnish with a lemon wedge and 2 honey sticks. The sipper will open the honey sticks and pour the contents into the drink. Include a short straw for stirring.

Don't chuckle over this seemingly unlikely combination of ingredients until you've tried it. It's summer in a glass.

2 bottles cold Wild Blue blueberry lager
1 can (12-ounce) frozen Minute Maid pink lemonade (defrosted, but no water
    added)
2 ounces blueberry-infused bourbon
10 ounces water
2 lemons cut into 12 wedges
1 cup fresh blueberries

Into a 1½–2 quart glass pitcher, pour the bottles of beer. Add lemonade, bourbon, and water; stir. After the foam subsides, squeeze and drop in the lemon wedges. Stir. Add ice and blueberries. Stir again. Serve over ice.

BLOOD ORANGE BOURBON

2 ounces blood orange–infused bourbon
½ ounce brown sugar syrup
4 dashes Fee Brothers West Indian orange bitters
1 ounce juice from a blood orange or a regular juice orange

Combine and shake over ice; strain into a chilled Martini glass. Float a thin round of orange on top to garnish.

BOURBON SHAKE UP

2 ounces Kentucky bourbon of your choice
1 ounce simple syrup
1 whole lemon cut into 4 wedges
1 ounce water

Combine bourbon and simple syrup in the glass. Squeeze and drop in the lemon wedges and water. Shake, shake, shake, shake! (Ah, if only they would serve these at the Kentucky State Fair. . . .)

BOURJITO

This was my answer to the Mojito craze of a few years back.

1 ounce brown sugar syrup
6 small lemon wedges
6 mint leaves
1 ounce limoncello
2 ounces Kentucky bourbon of your choice
3–4 ounces club soda

In a pint glass, place sugar syrup. Squeeze and drop in the lemon wedges, mint leaves, and limoncello. Muddle slightly. Add the bourbon and fill with ice. Shake and add more ice if needed. Top with club soda and stir. Garnish with a sprig of fresh mint and a lemon wedge on the rim. Serve with a long straw.

CATFISH HOUSE PUNCH

This is my version of the fish house punch that's been around since the 1730s. It's a strong but surprisingly good drink. Kentuckians enjoy angling for and eating catfish, hence the name.

½ cup brown sugar syrup
½ cup lemon juice
2 cups cooled fresh tea
1½ cups Kentucky bourbon (80–90 proof)
½ cup peach brandy
¼ cup Cruzan gold rum
¼ cup DeKuyper Peachtree schnapps
12–15 lemon wheels
pineapple wedges (optional)

In a 1½–2 quart glass pitcher or punch bowl, combine and stir all ingredients. Add ice and lemon wheels. Serve in glass or silver punch cups. Pineapple wedges make a nice addition.

EASY TROPICALE

This is the quick version of my award-winning Tropicale.

1 part Kentucky bourbon (80–90 proof)
1 part Cruzan coconut rum
1 part Tuaca
1 part brown sugar syrup
3 parts pineapple juice

Combine and shake over ice. Sprinkle with nutmeg and garnish with a fresh pineapple wedge and a cherry. Serve with a long straw.

KENTUCKY BOURBON PEACH CIDER

I admit that I've been able to find peach cider only in Georgia, but if you can find some (or have a friend in Georgia who can send you some), you'll love this cocktail.

1½ ounces Kentucky bourbon (80–90 proof)
½ ounce brown sugar syrup
4 ounces chilled peach cider

Combine in a glass and stir gently. Garnish with a stemmed red cherry dropped in the drink.

KENTUCKY BOURBON PLANTER'S PUNCH

Bourbon stands in for the traditional West Indian rum here.

2 ounces Kentucky bourbon (80–90 proof)
2 ounces brown sugar syrup
1 ounce fresh lemon juice
6 dashes Angostura bitters
5 ounces water
½ ounce 100-proof bourbon

In a pint glass filled with ice, shake all ingredients except the 100-proof bourbon. Add more ice if needed and float the 100-proof bourbon on top. Sprinkle with nutmeg. Garnish with a lemon wedge and a sprig of fresh mint. Serve with a long straw.

LOUISVILLE ICED BOURBON COFFEE

1½ ounces Kentucky bourbon (80–90 proof)
1 ounce brown sugar syrup
1 ounce Kahlua
5 ounces chilled coffee
1 ounce Baileys Irish Cream

Combine all ingredients except the Baileys in the glass over ice. Shake in a Boston shaker. Float the Baileys on top and serve with a long straw.

This drink honors the Cumberland Falls in southeastern Kentucky, one of only two places in the world (Victoria Falls in Africa is the other) where a moonbow of light regularly appears in the mist during a full moon. The Moonbow is light, misty, and perfect to drink on a night with a full moon.

2 ounces Kentucky bourbon (80–90 proof)
1 tablespoon simple syrup
1 tablespoon fresh orange juice
1 tablespoon fresh lime juice
2 ounces ginger ale
1 ounce cranberry juice

Combine bourbon, simple syrup, and citrus juices in the glass. Add ice and shake. Add ginger ale and stir. Add more ice if needed and float the cranberry juice on top.

I think of this drink as history in a glass. Sourwood honey is used in magic love spells in the Appalachian mountains, mint is a traditional folk medicine, and wild strawberries are common in summer.

2 tablespoons Kentucky sourwood honey dissolved in 2 tablespoons hot
    water and cooled
3–5 mint leaves
3 small strawberries, stemmed and cut in half
2 ounces Kentucky bourbon (80–90 proof)

Put the honey syrup, mint leaves, and strawberries in the glass and muddle lightly. Add ice and bourbon; shake. Garnish the rim with a slice of star fruit and a large stemmed strawberry into which has been stuck a mint sprig.

RUBY RED SOUR

2 ounces grapefruit-infused bourbon
1 tablespoon brown sugar syrup
1 tablespoon juice of a fresh ruby red grapefruit
4 dashes Fee Brothers grapefruit bitters

Combine, shake over ice, and strain into a chilled glass. Garnish with a stemmed red cherry.

SWEET PEACH TEA

2 large lemon wedges
2 ounces peach-infused bourbon
1 ounce simple syrup
6 ounces good brewed tea, cooled

Into the glass filled with ice, squeeze and drop the lemon wedges and add all other ingredients. Shake. Garnish with a large peach wedge and a sprig of lemon mint. Serve with a long straw.

WOOD ROSE

Wood rose grows in the tropics. Its flowers look like dried roses with translucent beige petals and large brownish-black seed pods. I discovered the plant when I lived in St. Croix. The drink's color reminds me of the plant. I use a bourbon brand whose name echoes the plant's name.

1 part Woodford Reserve bourbon
1 part Tuaca
1 part Chambord

Combine all ingredients and shake over ice; strain into a chilled glass. Garnish with 3 fresh raspberries dropped in the glass.

AUTUMN DRINKS

Included in this section are my recipes for taking off that first autumn chill, for sipping while cheering on your favorite local sports team, and for treating yourself after handing out the Halloween candy to the neighborhood goblins.

Note: For the apple cider called for in many recipes, buy the kind available for a few short weeks in the fall from local orchards. You can also find it in neighborhood groceries and produce markets.

Many craft brewers across the country, from Maine to California, are experimenting with aging stout in used bourbon barrels and bottling bourbon stout. In fact, it's now an official, judged style at the annual Great American Beer Festival in Denver, Colorado. Louisville's Bluegrass Brewing Company makes Jefferson Reserve Stout, aged in Jefferson Reserve barrels. For more information, go to www.bbcbrew.com.

22-ounce bottle of bourbon stout, chilled
3 ounces apple-pear-spice–infused bourbon
1 can (12 ounces) frozen apple juice, defrosted (do not add water)
1 cup fresh apple cider, chilled
1 cup chopped apples and pears

Combine all ingredients except apples and pears in a 2-quart stoneware pitcher; stir. Add ice and the chopped apples and pears.

I recommend Louisville Stoneware pitchers and mugs. Susan likes Mary Alice ("Ma") Hadley stoneware. Both stoneware lines are handsome, versatile products made in Louisville.

HOT AUTUMN CIDER

5 ounces fresh apple cider, heated
2 ounces apple-pear-spice–infused bourbon
1 tablespoon brown sugar syrup

Pour hot cider into a stoneware mug; add bourbon and brown sugar syrup. Stir; garnish with a cinnamon stick.

HOT KENTUCKY BOURBON CIDER

This is a great drink to store in a thermos and take along to a fall picnic or tailgate party.

4 ounces hot fresh apple cider
2 ounces Kentucky bourbon (80–90 proof)
1 ounce brown sugar syrup

Pour apple cider into a large heat-proof mug. Add bourbon and syrup; stir. Garnish with a large seeded apple slice and a sprinkle of cinnamon.

JOHN APPLESEED

1 part Kentucky bourbon (80–90 proof)
1 part DeKuyper red apple liqueur
1 part cranberry juice
2 parts non-alcoholic sparkling apple cider

Shake the bourbon, apple liqueur, and cranberry juice over ice and strain into a chilled champagne flute. Add apple cider and garnish with a red apple slice on the rim.

Go Team!

The next two drinks are ones I created to help fuel the intense rivalry between the University of Kentucky and University of Louisville sports teams. Annual matchups are played by the Wildcats and the Cardinals in both football and basketball.

BIG BLUE

1 ounce Kentucky bourbon (80–90 proof)
½ ounce blue curaçao
½ ounce sweet and sour mix

Combine over ice, shake, and strain into a shot glass.

BIG RED

1 ounce Kentucky bourbon (80–90 proof)
½ ounce DeKuyper Wild Strawberry liqueur
½ ounce sweet and sour mix

Combine over ice, shake, and strain into a shot glass.

Spooky Sips

These are for trick-or-treaters—age 21 and older, please.

GHOST IN THE GLASS

1½ ounces Kentucky bourbon of your choice
¾ ounce Godiva chocolate liqueur
1 ounce Baileys Irish Cream
dark chocolate syrup (the kind that creates a "shell" over ice cream)

On the inside of a chilled Martini glass, draw a ghost shape or two with the chocolate syrup. Shake the other ingredients over ice and strain into the glass. Garnish with a Peep's marshmallow ghost on the rim.

GREEN DEMON

1½ ounces Kentucky bourbon of your choice
1½ ounces Dumante pistachio liqueur
1 ounce Baileys Irish Cream
few drops of green food coloring

Combine, shake over ice, and strain into a chilled Martini glass. Garnish with a green gummy worm.

MOONSHINE

1½ ounces Kentucky bourbon of your choice
¾ ounce Hiram Walker mango liqueur
¾ ounce limoncello
¾ ounce triple sec

Combine over ice and strain into a chilled glass. Garnish with a thin slice of lemon floated on top.

WINTER DRINKS

During that dark period in American history known as Prohibition, a handful of distilleries were allowed to make bourbon "for medicinal purposes." (In fact, that's why you still see liquor sold in many Kentucky drug stores, a phenomenon often commented on by visitors to the Bluegrass State.) In this spirit, we include my recipes for hot drinks that will cure whatever ails you and, if you're not sick, will keep the germs at bay.

You'll also find many recipes suitable for winter holiday entertaining—Thanksgiving, Christmas, New Year's Eve, and Valentine's Day. The eggnog used in many recipes is stocked in grocery dairy cases during the holiday season.

FEEL BETTER KENTUCKY BOURBON TODDY

6 ounces boiling water
2 ounces Kentucky bourbon of your choice
1 ounce brown sugar syrup or undiluted Kentucky sourwood honey
4 dashes Angostura bitters
1 ounce fresh orange juice
1 ounce fresh lemon juice
1 ounce fresh lime juice

Pour boiling water into a heat-proof mug, add all other ingredients, and stir well. This is the perfect drink if you feel a cold coming on. If taken just before bedtime, use a high-alcohol, barrel-proof bourbon. Sweet dreams!

HOTTY TODDY

6 ounces boiling water
2 ounces spice-infused bourbon
¾ ounce brown sugar syrup
½ ounce fresh lemon juice
large lemon twist

Pour boiling water into a heat-proof mug. Add the other ingredients and serve with a straw. Drink while sitting in your favorite armchair by the fireplace.

KENTUCKY COFFEE

2 ounces Kentucky bourbon (80–90 proof)
¾ ounce brown sugar syrup
6 ounces hot black coffee
fresh whipped cream

Pour the bourbon and syrup into a large heat-proof mug. Add coffee and stir. Top with whipped cream on which you drizzle more brown sugar syrup; sprinkle with nutmeg. Serve with a straw.

Thanksgiving and Christmas Drinks

HOT BUTTERED BOURBON

5 ounces hot water
2 ounces spice-infused bourbon
¾ ounce brown sugar syrup
1 ounce butter at room temperature (No butter substitutes!)

Into a heat-proof mug, pour hot water, bourbon, and syrup. Stir well. Add the butter and stir rapidly to mix the butter into the liquid.

CANDY CANE

This is my contribution to the bartending trend of using hard candy in cocktails. It has a beautiful red color and a hint of vanilla in the taste.

3 ounces candy cane–infused bourbon

Shake over ice and strain into a chilled Martini glass. Garnish by hanging a miniature candy cane on the rim.

CANDY CANE EGGNOG

1 ounce candy cane–infused bourbon
3 ounces ready-to-drink eggnog

Combine and shake (no ice) and pour into a white wine glass. Top with whipped cream, grated nutmeg, and a miniature candy cane. Serve with two short straws.

CHRISTMAS PUNCH

1 ounce spice-infused bourbon
1 teaspoon brown sugar syrup
squeeze of lemon juice
1 ounce fresh orange juice
1 ounce cranberry juice
1 ounce sparkling wine

Combine all ingredients except the sparkling wine over ice, and shake. Strain into a champagne flute and top with the wine. Drop fresh cranberries in the drink to garnish.

CHOCOLATE EGGNOG

1 ounce spice-infused bourbon
½ ounce Godiva chocolate liqueur
3 ounces ready-to-drink eggnog

Combine ingredients and shake (no ice); pour into a white wine glass. Top with whipped cream, grated nutmeg, and a miniature candy cane. Serve with two short straws.

*Eggnogs. Left to right: Candy Cane,
Traditional, and Pistachio.*

PISTACHIO EGGNOG

1 ounce spice-infused bourbon
½ ounce Dumante pistachio liqueur
3 ounces ready-to-drink eggnog
2–3 drops green food coloring

Combine ingredients and shake (no ice); pour into a white wine glass. Top with whipped cream, grated nutmeg, and a miniature candy cane. Serve with two short straws.

POINSETTIA

1 part Kentucky bourbon (80–90 proof)
1 part DeKuyper pomegranate liqueur
1 part brown sugar syrup

Shake over ice and strain into a chilled Martini glass. Garnish with a lemon wedge dropped into the drink.

Pumpkin Eggnog in a punch bowl.

PUMPKIN EGGNOG

4 ounces brown sugar syrup
1 can (8 ounces) pumpkin
    puree (*not* pumpkin pie mix)
1 ounce spice-infused
    bourbon
3 ounces ready-to-drink
    eggnog

Stir brown sugar syrup into
canned pumpkin puree. Keep
refrigerated in a jar with a lid.
Combine 2 ounces of the pumpkin
mix with bourbon and eggnog.
Shake (no ice). Pour into a white
wine glass. Top with whipped
cream, grated nutmeg, and a
miniature candy cane. Serve with
two short straws.

TRADITIONAL EGGNOG

1 ounce spice-infused bourbon
3 ounces ready-to-drink eggnog
brown sugar syrup to taste

Combine ingredients and shake (no ice); pour into a white wine glass. Top with whipped cream, grated nutmeg, and a miniature candy cane. Serve with two short straws.

New Year's Eve

KENTUCKY BOURBON SPARKLER

1 ounce bourbon
½ ounce brown sugar syrup
½ ounce Tuaca
4 ounces sparkling wine

Combine bourbon, syrup, and Tuaca in a champagne flute. Stir and add sparkling wine. Stir again and garnish with an orange twist.

Valentine's Day

CHOCOLATE CINNAMON HEART

1½ ounces cinnamon-infused bourbon
1 ounce Tuaca
½ ounce brown sugar syrup
1 ounce Godiva chocolate liqueur

Shake all ingredients over ice and strain into a chilled Martini glass. Garnish with a cherry dipped in dark chocolate.

STRAWBERRY LOVE BITES

3 large strawberries
coarse brown sugar (Bourbon Barrel Foods Vanilla Sugar is excellent.)
1 ounce strawberry-infused bourbon
½ ounce brown sugar syrup
1 ounce caramel sauce, honey, or Bourbon Barrel Vanilla Sorghum
1 teaspoon toasted, chopped almonds
½ ounce Tuaca

Remove the stems from the strawberries and hollow them out to hold the drink. Dip the rims in the coarse brown sugar. Put the caramel (or other) sauce into a large Martini glass and sprinkle the remaining brown sugar and almonds on top. Carefully place the strawberries in the glass. Shake the bourbon, brown sugar syrup, and Tuaca over ice and pour into the strawberries. Garnish with a fresh mint sprig and serve with small sipping straws and a small spoon.

CHAPTER SIX

The Sweet Side of Bourbon

TIKI DRINKS

Yes, they're back. You may not have a Trader Vic's in your town, but tiki drinks are enjoying a vogue for summertime sipping. Since both bourbon and rum are on the sweet side, I'm perfectly happy to use bourbon in place of rum in many of my libation creations.

BOOTLEGGER

My father was a rumrunner and my Granmom was a bootlegger. He brought it in and she sold it, and that's how my parents met. Hence me. A Rumrunner was a popular drink a few years ago and it made me think of my family. Granny, this one's for you!

1½ ounces Kentucky bourbon (80–90 proof)
1 ounce Cruzan banana rum
1 ounce blackberry brandy
½ ounce Rose's lime juice
½ ounce grenadine

Shake all ingredients over ice in a large Old Fashioned glass. Garnish with banana slices and fresh blackberries.

KENTUCKY BOURBON TIKI PUNCH

Bourbon stands in for the rum in this classic West Indian punch.

2 ounces Kentucky bourbon (80–90 proof)
½ ounce brown sugar syrup
3 ounces fresh orange juice
3 ounces pineapple juice
½ ounce grenadine

To a pint glass filled with ice, add bourbon, brown sugar syrup, orange juice, and pineapple juice. Shake. Add more ice if needed; drizzle with grenadine and sprinkle nutmeg on top. Garnish with an orange slice and a cherry and serve with a long straw.

KENTUCKY HAWAIIAN PUNCH

This reminds me of a certain canned fruit punch my kids loved to drink. But this version is all grown up, just like my kids.

1 ounce Kentucky bourbon (80–90 proof)
1 ounce vodka
1 ounce Southern Comfort
1 ounce grenadine
2 ounces fresh orange juice

Combine all ingredients over ice in a tall glass and shake. No garnish.

KENTUCKY MAI TAI

1½ ounces Kentucky bourbon (80–90 proof)
1 ounce Amaretto Di Saronno
1 ounce triple sec
1 ounce fresh orange juice
1 teaspoon fresh lime juice
1 tablespoon grenadine

Combine all ingredients and shake over ice. Strain into a chilled Martini glass. Garnish with a pineapple wedge, lime wheel, cherry, and—naturally—a paper umbrella.

KENTUCKY MAMA

2 ounces Kentucky bourbon (80–90 proof)
1 ounce coconut rum
1 ounce fresh orange juice
1 ounce pineapple juice
½ ounce grenadine

Combine all ingredients and shake over ice in a tall glass. Garnish with an orange wheel, a fresh pineapple wedge, and a cherry. Serve with a long straw.

KENTUCKY SCORPION

1½ ounces Kentucky bourbon (80–90 proof)
¾ ounce brandy
1 ounce Amaretto Di Saronno
1 tablespoon fresh lemon juice
1 tablespoon simple syrup
2 ounces fresh orange juice

Shake all ingredients over ice in a large Old Fashioned glass. Garnish with a large lemon twist, an orange wheel, and a cherry.

LIVING DEAD (*OR* KENTUCKY ZOMBIE)

The 1985 zombie movie Return of the Living Dead *was set in Louisville (though it was actually filmed in California). So this is the drink to have with popcorn when watching your collection of classic zombie movies.*

1½ ounces Kentucky bourbon (80–90 proof)
¾ ounce DeKuyper pomegranate liqueur
¾ ounce pineapple juice
½ ounce lime juice
½ ounce brown sugar syrup
¾ ounce Southern Comfort
½ ounce brandy
½ ounce 100-proof Kentucky bourbon

Combine all ingredients except the 100-proof bourbon in a tall glass with ice. Shake. Float the 100-proof bourbon on top. Garnish with a mint sprig, a pineapple wedge, an orange wheel, and a cherry. Serve with a long straw.

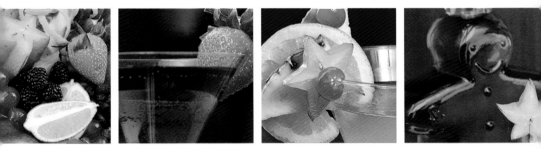

This is the Bluegrass version of a popular Bahamas drink.

1½ ounces Kentucky bourbon (80–90 proof)
1 ounce Cruzan coconut rum
1 ounce Cruzan pineapple rum
1 ounce Hiram Walker mango liqueur
1 ounce pineapple juice

Shake all ingredients over ice in a large Old Fashioned glass. Garnish with an orange wheel, a pineapple wedge, and a cherry.

DESSERT DRINKS

These are sure to please a grown-up's sweet tooth. You'll need a blender to execute the frozen recipes.

DERBY PIE SHAKE

Derby Pie®, a traditional chocolate-nut chess pie, is a registered trademark of Kern's Kitchen in Louisville. You can find the pie in the freezer case at many Louisville area groceries and liquor stores.

2 ounces Kentucky bourbon (80–90 proof)
1 ounce Godiva chocolate liqueur
1 ounce Nocello liqueur
1 thin slice Derby Pie®, broken into small pieces
3 scoops vanilla ice cream
whipped cream

Combine bourbon, chocolate liqueur, Nocello liqueur, and ice cream in a blender with a little ice, and whirl until you have a frozen slurry. Pour into a chilled pint glass. Garnish with whipped cream, a few mini chocolate chips, a cherry, and a thin slice of Derby Pie®. Serve with a long straw.

KENTUCKY BOURBON BANANAS STEPHEN FOSTER

2 ounces Kentucky bourbon (80–90 proof)
¼ teaspoon cinnamon
1 ounce Cruzan banana rum
1 ounce brown sugar syrup
2 ripe bananas, peeled and cut in thirds
1 cup ice

Put in a blender the bourbon, cinnamon, rum, brown sugar syrup, and bananas, reserving one slice of banana for garnish. Add the ice on top, and whirl. Pour into a large wine glass. Garnish with the slice of banana and sprinkle a little cinnamon on top. Serve with a long straw.

KENTUCKY BOURBON FUDGE NUTTY

2 ounces Kentucky bourbon (80–90 proof)
1 ounce Godiva chocolate liqueur
½ ounce Frangelico
½ ounce praline liqueur

Combine all ingredients over ice, shake, and strain into a chilled glass. (Coating the inside of the glass with melted chocolate first is a nice touch.) Garnish with a cherry dipped in chocolate on a pick.

JUJU CORN COCKTAIL

Jujus, products of traditional mountain magic, were dolls made from dried gourds and ears of corn. They were hung over illegal stills to protect the moonshine from the revenuers.

1 ounce Kentucky bourbon (80–90 proof)
½ ounce Tuaca
½ ounce DeKuyper ButterShots schnapps
½ ounce Baileys Irish Cream

Shake all ingredients over ice and pour into a large shot glass.

PEACHES & CREAM

2 ounces Kentucky bourbon (80–90 proof)
1 ounce brown sugar syrup
1 ounce Southern Comfort
1 ounce Baileys Irish Cream
2 ripe peaches, peeled and sliced
1 cup ice

Put all ingredients except ice in a blender, reserving one large slice of peach for garnish. Add the ice on top, and whirl. Pour into a large wine glass. Garnish with reserved peach slice and serve with a long straw.

PINEAPPLE WHIP

I was inspired to make this drink by the (non-alcoholic) pineapple whip that's a mainstay of the Kentucky State Fair.

2 ounces Kentucky bourbon (80–90 proof)
1 ounce brown sugar syrup
1 ounce Cruzan pineapple rum
1 cup fresh pineapple, peeled and cut into small pieces
1 cup ice

Put all ingredients except ice in a blender, reserving one pineapple wedge for garnish. Add the ice on top, and whirl. Pour into a large wine glass. Garnish with a cherry and reserved pineapple wedge. Serve with a long straw.

SNOWFLAKE

2 ounces Kentucky bourbon (80–90 proof)
4 tablespoons Coco Lopez cream of coconut
1 ounce Cruzan coconut rum
1/8 teaspoon ground cloves
1 tablespoon brown sugar syrup
1 cup ice

Put all ingredients in a blender and whirl. Dip the rim of a chilled Martini glass in simple syrup and then in shredded coconut. Pour the drink into the glass and serve.

STRAWBERRY DELIGHT

2 ounces Kentucky bourbon (80–90 proof)
1 ounce Amaretto Di Saronno
1 ounce brown sugar syrup
1 ounce Smucker's strawberry syrup
1 cup sliced ripe strawberries
1 cup ice

Put all ingredients in a blender, reserving 1 large whole strawberry, and whirl. Pour into a large wine glass. Garnish with the whole strawberry on the rim. Serve with a long straw.

TOFFEE BAR

1 ounce Kentucky bourbon (80–90 proof)
½ ounce praline liqueur
½ ounce Kahlua
½ ounce DeKuyper ButterShots schnapps
½ ounce Baileys Irish Cream

Combine all ingredients over ice in a large Old Fashioned glass, and shake.

CHAPTER SEVEN

Guest Cocktails

I'm proud to be a member of the community of bourbon enthusiasts who love creating new bourbon drinks—a community that includes distillers, restaurateurs, other bartenders, and Jack's customers. Here I've invited several of my friends to submit their recipes for bourbon cocktails in hopes they'll inspire you to create your own.

JOANNA GOLDSTEIN'S BOURBON SIDECAR

Susan: *Joanna and I go to dinner at Jack's every Tuesday night after the rehearsal of the Indiana University Southeast Orchestra. (Joanna is the conductor and I play trumpet.) She'd tried a bourbon version of the classic cognac sidecar made by a colleague and asked Joy to make one for her. The following drink was the delicious result.*

(Bourbon Sidecar, continued)

2½ ounces Old Forester
½ ounce triple sec
splash of sweet and sour mix
squeeze of lemon

Shake all ingredients over ice and strain into a chilled Martini glass with a sugared rim. Garnish with a slice of orange.

NANCY SHEPHERD'S BOURBON COCKTAIL

I've been making this drink for Nancy (owner of Louisville's Café Metro and Uptown Café) for twenty years. Nancy told me that one night two priests from Columbus, Indiana, came into Café Metro and ordered a bourbon cocktail. They said this was how it was made. Nancy's been drinking it ever since.

2 ounces Kentucky bourbon
¼ ounce triple sec
¼ ounce Benedictine
large lemon wedge

Shake the liquid ingredients over ice. Squeeze and drop in the lemon wedge. Strain into a chilled Martini glass and garnish with a lemon twist.

PROOF'S SIGNATURE DARKENED MANHATTAN

Proof is the bourbon-centric restaurant and bar located in Louisville's 21C Hotel. This cocktail is the creation of Michael Bonadies, president and CEO of the hotel.

1½ ounces Woodford Reserve bourbon
1 ounce sweet vermouth
1 ounce Starbucks coffee liqueur

Shake all ingredients over ice and strain into a chilled Martini glass. Garnish with a cherry.

WOODFORD AND GINGER

This recipe comes from Tim Laird, CEO (Chief Entertaining Officer) of Louisville distiller Brown-Forman. Tim travels all over the country to promote Woodford Reserve and give workshops on home entertaining. He has never met a stranger.

1½ ounces Woodford Reserve bourbon
1¾ ounces simple syrup
1 ounce fresh lime juice
¼ teaspoon ground ginger
club soda

In a shaker glass with ice, combine Woodford Reserve, simple syrup, lime juice, and ground ginger. Shake and strain into a tall glass with ice. Top with club soda. Garnish with slices of fresh ginger root.

BOURBON BLACKBERRY SMASH

Another from Tim Laird.

6 fresh blackberries
leaves of one fresh sprig of rosemary

¾ ounce simple syrup
1½ ounces Woodford Reserve bourbon
2 ounces ginger ale

Muddle 5 of the blackberries and the rosemary leaves in a mixing glass. Add simple syrup and Woodford Reserve. Shake and strain into an Old Fashioned glass. Top with ginger ale and garnish with the remaining blackberry.

BILL SAMUELS' NO NAME YET (But So Good!) COCKTAIL

Bill Samuels Jr. is the president of Maker's Mark, the classic wheated bourbon with the trademark bottle dipped in red wax. His family has been distilling distinctive bourbons for generations.

1¼ ounces Maker's Mark bourbon
½ ounce honey syrup (equal parts honey and water)
fresh grapefruit juice
sprig of fresh mint

Into an Old Fashioned glass filled with ice, pour the Maker's Mark and honey syrup. Fill with grapefruit juice and garnish with the mint (optional).

PRESTON VAN WINKLE'S OLD FASHIONED

Preston Van Winkle, great-grandson of Pappy Van Winkle, is famous for his Old Fashioneds and kindly provided this recipe, as well as the one for his fruity Bourbon Berry.

1½ ounces Van Winkle 15-year-old bourbon
1 orange slice
2 brown sugar cubes soaked in orange bitters and Angostura bitters

Muddle the orange slice and sugar cubes in the bottom of the glass. Stir gently while slowly adding bourbon and ice. Garnish with a twist of orange and a fresh cherry.

BOURBON BERRY

1½ ounces Van Winkle 10-year-old bourbon
3 teaspoons honey-water (made by adding one splash of water to 2 teaspoons honey)
¾ ounce blackberry puree
¾ ounce green apple puree
2 teaspoons vanilla sugar
¾ ounce fresh lemon juice
1 tablespoon crème de myrtille (blueberry) liqueur

Shake and strain all ingredients except the blueberry liqueur into the glass over crushed ice. Float the liqueur on top of the drink.

SEELBACH COCKTAIL

This cocktail was created at Louisville's Seelbach Hotel, circa 1917, but the recipe was lost, probably during Prohibition, and the drink didn't see the light of day again until 1995, when a hotel manager rediscovered the formula. It's an unusual drink, as it calls for two brands of bitters, Angostura and Peychaud's. Current Seelbach manager Mark Butcher provided the recipe.

1½ ounces bourbon
1½ ounces Cointreau
7 dashes Angostura bitters
7 dashes Peychaud's bitters
4 ounces chilled brut champagne

Pour all ingredients, in the order listed, into a champagne flute. Add an orange twist as garnish.

CARAMEL APPLE MARTINI

Many thanks to Angela H. Traver of Buffalo Trace Distillery for this and the following refreshing bourbon cocktails.

Two parts Buffalo Trace bourbon
1 part praline liqueur
1 part DeKuyper Apple Pucker schnapps

Shake all ingredients over ice and serve in a chilled Martini glass. Garnish with a slice of green apple.

KENTUCKY MIMOSA

¾ ounce Buffalo Trace bourbon
1 ounce sparkling apple cider
ginger ale

Add the ingredients to the glass in the order listed, and serve.

KENTUCKY BRUNCH

The busy bees at Jim Beam Distillery, who make a multitude of bourbon brands, sent us several cocktail recipes. We especially enjoyed this one and the three that follow.

1½ ounces Jim Beam White Label bourbon
¾ ounce DeKuyper triple sec
2 ounces fresh sweet and sour mix
1 heaping bar spoon (about 1 teaspoon) of orange marmalade

Shake all ingredients with ice and strain into a chilled glass. Garnish with an orange slice on the rim.

LEGAL AIDE

1½ ounces Knob Creek bourbon
¾ ounce DeKuyper Peachtree schnapps
1 ounce fresh sweet and sour mix
1 ounce guava puree
¼ ounce grenadine

Shake all ingredients with ice until well blended. Strain into a chilled glass. Garnish with a flamed orange peel.

KENTUCKY LEMON DROP $\quad\Y$

1½ ounces Basil Hayden bourbon
¾ ounce limoncello
2 ounces fresh sweet and sour mix
5–6 fresh spearmint leaves

Shake all ingredients with ice until well blended. Strain into a chilled glass with a sugared rim (optional). Garnish with a lemon wheel. The little pieces of mint that will be floating around in the cocktail are little bursts of flavor; it's considered good luck if you get one.

THE FIG THING

1½ ounces Jim Beam Black Label
½ ounce Harvey's Bristol Cream
1½ ounces fresh sweet and sour mix
1 ounce apple juice
1 mission fig marinated in bourbon
½ ounce egg white

In a mixing glass, muddle the fig, add the remaining ingredients, and shake vigorously with ice. Strain into a chilled glass and garnish with fresh ground nutmeg.

ROSÉ RITA

The architecture of the Four Roses Distillery in Lawrenceberg, Kentucky, is Spanish Mission, so it's fitting to include a bourbon-based twist on a favorite South-of-the-Border drink.

2 ounces Margarita mix
1 ounce Four Roses bourbon
dash of grenadine

Add the mix to the bourbon and shake over ice. Pour into a chilled glass. Add a dash of grenadine, but do not mix. The red of the grenadine will settle near the bottom of the glass for a nice multicolor effect. Garnish with two maraschino cherries.

CHAPTER EIGHT

Nibbles

As we've said before, this book is intended as a guide for the home bartender. Now that you've mastered the mixing of the drinks, you may want some suggestions about finger food to accompany your bourbon-based sippage. Since bourbon is characteristically on the sweet side, you'll find that a variety of savory foods make good complements to the drinks. And just as bourbon is a traditional Kentucky and southern drink, the traditional food ingredients of the region pair naturally with the beverage. So think about corn (bourbon's main ingredient, after all), pork, and chicken, all plentiful in southern cooking, as starting points for your party food. You don't have to spend a lot of time in the kitchen whipping up treats. Keep it simple.

QUICK BITES

Among the prepared snacks that you can just pour into attractive bowls and place around the room are:

Nuts, especially roasted and salted almonds and pecans
Goldfish® crackers, any favorite flavors
Cheese straws
Cheese (sharp ones such as cheddar) and crackers
Corn chips with salsa or bean dip
Popcorn

Here's a tip about popcorn. You can, of course, be high tech and use the microwave variety. But low tech yields some wonderful flavors. Pop popcorn from a jar in a heavy, lidded saucepan. Cover the bottom with a film of corn oil, heat on medium high until a test kernel pops, then add a single layer of kernels to cover the bottom. When popped, empty into a large bowl and add salt and melted butter. Dried dill is another nice touch. For a truly southern touch, use melted bacon drippings instead of corn oil. This imparts a subtle bacony flavor and you won't need to add butter after popping. (Susan keeps her bacon drippings in a stoneware mug in the fridge and always makes popcorn this way.)

TOOTHPICK TREATS

Many grocery meat counters, as well as local butchers, feature sausages in a variety of flavors. The quarter-pound links can be cooked and then sliced into bites and served with toothpicks. Consider varieties such as spicy chorizo (pork or chicken), chicken-apple, pork with garlic, and chicken-cilantro. You may want to save traditional sage-flavored sausage for breakfast with your pancakes covered in bourbon-laced maple syrup.

Other toothpick-stabbed bites can include anything you fancy wrapped in cooked bacon, such as water chestnuts, shrimp, scallops, or bite-size pieces of roasted chicken breast or turkey. Chicken wings (which have their own built in "toothpicks") would be tasty with your cocktails, but there's always the awkward problem of what to do with the bones.

FINGER SANDWICHES

Again, do the easy thing. Buy cocktail buns to make sandwiches using any of the following:

Pulled pork, chicken, or beef, obtained from your favorite local barbecue
   joint
Sliced pork tenderloin

Sliced roast beef or beef tenderloin
Country ham
Baked ham
Pimiento cheese

A little barbecue sauce on the pulled meats would be good. Try a dollop of steak sauce with the sliced beef and pork. Ham can be dressed with mayonnaise or, even better, Durkee's® sauce. For an authentic taste of Louisville, use Henry Bain sauce (below) in place of steak sauce. For yet another Louisville flavor, serve Benedictine spread (below) on party-size slices of pumpernickel bread. (Bourbon will make the spread disappear if you serve it on white bread.)

RECIPES FOR SAUCES AND SPREADS

If you really want to spend some time in the kitchen, here are some classics that you could easily find in Louisville but are such local foods that you will need to make your own if you don't live in the Derby City.

BENEDICTINE

This local favorite was invented by caterer and restaurateur Jennie Benedict, who had a tearoom in downtown Louisville in the first half of the twentieth century. This recipe is modified from Benedict's 1922 Blue Ribbon Cookbook (Reprint: Lexington: University Press of Kentucky, 2008).

16 ounces cream cheese, softened
6 tablespoons cucumber juice
2 tablespoon onion juice
2 teaspoons salt
dash of cayenne pepper
4–5 drops green food coloring

To get the juice, peel and grate a cucumber, then wrap it in several layers of cheesecloth and squeeze the juice into a dish. Do the same for the onion (or buy bottled onion juice). Mix all ingredients with a fork until well blended. Don't use an electric mixer or food processor because the spread will be too runny. Makes a pound of spread.

HENRY BAIN SAUCE

Like the venerable Old Fashioned, this sauce was invented at Louisville's Pendennis Club. Henry Bain (1863–1928) was the club's African American headwaiter, and he's credited with inventing the sauce. This recipe, by former Courier-Journal *food editor Sarah Fritschner, was printed in the newspaper on February 19, 2007. In some sources, the pickled walnuts are not included, but they really are the key to the sauce's unique flavor.*

1 jar (17-ounce) Major Grey's chutney
half of a 9-ounce jar imported pickled walnuts
1 bottle (14-ounce) ketchup
1 bottle (11-ounce) A.1. steak sauce
1 bottle (10-ounce) Worcestershire sauce
1 bottle (12-ounce) chili sauce
Tabasco sauce, to taste

Put the chutney and walnuts, if using, in a blender and chop fine or puree as you prefer (you'll need to stop and stir). Combine with other ingredients and season to taste with Tabasco. Makes 4 pints. In addition to using it as a sandwich dressing, you can slather it on top of a block of cream cheese and serve as a cracker spread.

KENTUCKY SAUCE

Unlike other suggestions, this sauce is on the sweet, rather than savory, side. It's one of my favorites, and I suggest serving it on top of cream cheese spread on crackers, as you might the Henry Bain sauce. It's also terrific over vanilla ice cream. The recipe is from The Courier-Journal Cookbook *by Lillian Marshall (Louisville: Courier-Journal & Times, 1971).*

1 cup brown sugar
1 cup white sugar
1 cup water
1 cup pecans, broken
1 cup strawberry preserves
1 orange
1 lemon
1 cup bourbon

Combine sugars with water and cook until syrup reaches about 240 degrees on a candy thermometer, or until it will almost, but not quite, spin a thread. Remove from the heat and stir in pecans and preserves.

Remove the rind from the orange and lemon with a potato parer and chop fine. Cut off and discard the white membrane; remove sections. Cut the orange and lemon sections into small pieces. Add the cut-up rind, fruit, and bourbon to the sugar and water mixture. Set away in the refrigerator to ripen. Makes over a quart and keeps indefinitely.

GLOSSARY

You'll be able to "speak bourbon" like an expert when you know the language. These are the terms you will encounter on bourbon labels.

Aging: Bourbon must be aged in charred, never-before-used barrels traditionally made of white oak (*Quercus alba*) for at least two years. Most are aged between five and eight years.

Bourbon: Whiskey distilled from fermented grain. By law, at least 51 percent of the mash bill (grains used) must be corn. Other grains used are typically barley and rye in varying proportions. Wheat is sometimes used in place of rye; such whiskeys are called "wheated"bourbons. Maker's Mark and Old Fitzgerald are examples of wheated bourbons.

The name "bourbon" is said by some to come from Bourbon County, Kentucky, named to honor the French royal family that aided the American colonists during the War for Independence. But no one really knows for certain where the name came from.

Proof: Equal to twice the alcohol content by volume. Hence, an 86 proof bourbon is 43 percent alcohol. Proofs are adjusted by the addition of water after aging. A *barrel proof bourbon* has not been so adjusted. These are typically 110 proof and higher.

Single barrel: The bottling is all from one selected barrel.

Small batch: A limited production of bourbon using select, mixed barrels.

Sour mash: The soupy alcoholic liquid strained from the first distillation and added to the next batch of grain for distillation (rather like a sourdough starter). Also called "backset." Dr. James Crowe, a Scot who came to Kentucky in the nineteenth century, developed the technique to help keep bourbon consistent from one distillation to the next.

Straight bourbon whiskey: The legal definition of American bourbon says that "straight bourbon" is made up of at least 51 percent corn; is distilled at no more than 80 percent alcohol; is matured at no higher than 62.5 percent alcohol; and is matured in new charred oak barrels for no less than two years. It is bottled at a minimum of 40 percent alcohol by volume.

Whiskey (spelled "whisky" in Europe): An alcoholic beverage made from distilled grain. Bourbon is one of many whiskeys, including Scotch, Canadian, Irish, rye, Tennessee, and Kentucky whiskey. The last differs from bourbon in being aged in *used* charred oak barrels.

SUGGESTED FURTHER READING

These books will give you more information on cocktail mixing in general and bourbon and its history in particular. It is by no means an exhaustive list, but includes books that we like.

Broom, Dave. *New American Bartender's Handbook.* San Diego: Thunder Bay Press, 2003.

Carson, Gerald. *The Social History of Bourbon.* New York: Dodd, Mead, 1963.

Crowgey, Henry G. *Kentucky Bourbon: The Early Years of Whiskeymaking.* Lexington: University Press of Kentucky, 1971; reprint, 2008.

DeGroff, Dale. *The Craft of the Cocktail.* New York: Clarkson Potter, 2002.

Givens, Ron. *Bourbon at Its Best: The Lore & Allure of America's Finest Spirits.* Cincinnati: Clerisy Press, 2008.

Herbst, Sharon Tyler, and Herbst, Ron. *The Ultimate A-to-Z Bar Guide.* New York: Broadway Books, 1998.

Hellmich, Mittie. *Ultimate Bar Book: The Comprehensive Guide to Over 1,000 Cocktails.* San Francisco: Chronicle Books, 2006.

Jackson, Michael. *Whiskey: The Definitive World Guide.* London: Dorling Kindersley, 2005.

Murray, Jim. *Classic Bourbon, Tennessee & Rye Whiskey.* London: Prion, 1998.

Nickell, Col. Joe. *The Kentucky Mint Julep.* Lexington: University Press of Kentucky, 2003.

Poister, John J. *The New American Bartender's Guide.* New York: New American Library, 1999.

Regan, Gary. *The Joy of Mixology: The Consummate Guide to the Bartender's Craft.* New York: Clarkson Potter, 2003.

Regan, Gary, and Regan, Mardee Haidi. *The Book of Bourbon: And Other Fine American Whiskies.* Boston: Houghton Mifflin, 1998.

Thomas, Jerry. *The Bar-Tender's Guide: How to Mix Drinks* (reprint of the 1887 edition). Seattle: CreateSpace, 2008.

Williams, H. I. *3 Bottle Bar.* New York: M.S. Mill Co., 1946.

INDEX

ABOUT THE AUTHORS

Joy Perrine is a native of New Jersey, but that hasn't stopped her from developing an abiding love of Kentucky bourbon. She has been named "Best Bartender in Louisville" by *Louisville Magazine* and has won numerous awards for her cocktails. Articles about her and her drinks recipes have appeared in the *Courier-Journal*, *Saveur*, and *Food & Wine*, and at *www.southernfoodways.com*. She is the bar manager at Jack's Lounge and Equus Restaurant in Louisville.

Susan Reigler is an award-winning former restaurant critic and drinks writer for the *Courier-Journal*. Her articles about bourbon have been published in *Malt Advocate* and *Wine Enthusiast* as well as in several books about traveling in Kentucky. Her most recent book, *The Complete Guide to Kentucky State Parks*, is also published by the University Press of Kentucky.